Ruin

Ruin

CYNTHIA CRUZ

Alice James Books
Farmington, Maine

10 9 8 7 6 5 4 3 2 1

Alice James Books are published by Alice James Poetry Cooperative, Inc., an affiliate of the University of Maine at Farmington.

ALICE JAMES BOOKS
238 MAIN STREET
FARMINGTON, ME 04938

www.alicejamesbooks.org

LIBRARY OF CONGRESS CATALOGING-IN-PUBLICATION DATA
Cruz, Cynthia.
Ruin / Cynthia Cruz.
  p.   cm.
ISBN-13: 978–1–882295–58–6 (pbk.)
ISBN-10: 1–882295–58–7 (pbk.)
I. Title.
PS3603.R893R85 2006
811.'6–dc22   2006016285

Alice James Books gratefully acknowledges support from the University of Maine at Farmington and the National Endowment for the Arts. ❧

Cover Art: Mike Cockrill, *Journey*, 2006, oil on canvas, 72 x 52². Courtesy 31GRAND.

CONTENTS

Praying II

ACKNOWLEDGMENTS

Grateful acknowledgment is made to the editors of the following journals and anthologies in which these poems, sometimes under different titles or in slightly different versions, appeared:

AGNI: "F-Space"

American Poetry Review: "Door to Heaven II" and "Through the Night, Softly"

Bellevue Literary Review: "Prelude to 220, or 110"

Black Warrior Review: "You Will Be Like Your Dreams Tonight II"

Boston Review: "Microscopic Winter" and "Microscopic Winter II"

Colorado Review: "Through the Night, Softly II," "Door to Heaven," "Five-Day Locker," "Transfixed," "Joe the Lion II" and "Toby"

Columbia: "Self-Portrait in Froehlichia" and "The Report on Horses"

Grand Street: "Goleta," "Little Fox in Ghost-Weed," "Nepenthe," "The Kingdom" and "The Report on Horses II"

Paris Review: "January" and " Self-Portrait in Horsehair Wig"

Perihelion: "Texarkana"

The Iowa Anthology of New American Poetries, University of Iowa Press: "Self-Portrait in Froehlichia," " Shoot," " Shoot II," "Sparks, Nevada"

Isn't it Romantic: 100 Poems by Younger American Poets, Wave Books: "Self-Portrait in Horsehair Wig"

I also wish to thank the PUFFIN and PEN Foundations and Yaddo and the MacDowell Colony for their generous support.

In The Kingdom I

January

A California of snow and the surprise
Of illness. I throned myself in the white
Noise of its silence and watched as the world
Fell away. All the silver flickerings of possibility
Going out like the sound of horse hooves
Clicking into the distance. *It is almost*
The end. Anesthesia of medicine and me,
Beneath its warm bell of milk. My girlhood was
Microscopic: a locked window overlooking the
Sea. An atlas of the disaster: an un-lit hall and
A shift in the waves of the field. Blue bedside
Porcelain. Michelle, my little sister, silent as
A weed. I took all the things I loved and
Smashed them one by one.

Self-Portrait in Horsehair Wig

In the next life in an absinthe slip
Of ribbons, water-silk coat, glass seeds
Like water at the throat, I'll be adored
By a kneeling army of boys.
In a blue blood summer, you'll be criminal:
Clyde-like, dark-eyed and timid.
Your face will be of brilliant countenance.
There will be no dour consequence to our secret
Meeting. In the evening, we will be astonishing
As ever in perfect dress. In the room of
Hard-pasted porcelain and water clocks,
You'll press your slender fingers at the hinge,
Discover a hidden winter trapped in a snuffbox.

The Kingdom

We three girls in the Kingdom at the end
Our hands grasping out to mother.
Exquisite, in her Mandarin coat and lace-
Stitched satin pajamas. Every afternoon,
A myriad of allergy tests. Seaweed-green
Glass bottles filled with sleep: small black tablets and
The poking of needles up and down our backs.

The Report on Horses

Then, the final season of my brother's last visit.
His long dark hair in his face, and shirtsleeves
Concealing his thin white arms. Like a girl, he was always
Trading in what little he owned
Of his life. Already he was
Too fragile for the world.

In my mind I have been hiding
Among the ruinous thistle of last winter:
Fox, my girlhood horse, wasting away in the barn,
Her weak limbs at rest along the tremendous dark
Of her body.

The Report on Horses II

Then I was back at the old house, my brother
Still alive.

The two of us racing through the yellow sagebrush,
Dust rising from the earth like mother's

Drunk words, spies in the hallway.
Shadows in the orchard.

Billy's hand in mine, leading me into the wood.
A boy's, beginning, as if for the first time, *Come on,*

He said, *Let's find something still alive
Left to kill.*

Goleta

Lady Murasaki was mother's mare and Flying
Cloud was father's, his favorite, a pale strawberry roan.
Little Fox was mine, upon whose back I broke
Loose those locked rooms, that
House. The Ranch, Goleta,
The impossible fire. A field, a world, a winter
Of singing that would not stop. At night,
Even now, I can hear the sound
Of great flocks passing overhead.

Twelve in Yellow-Weed at the Edge

Then, the police arrive—they don't find me.
I'm disguised as a boy in a champagne wig
And hid inside the gold rattle of a warm Appalachia wind.
Beneath the trash of willow, I am. The sorrow
Of trailer parks and carnie uncles. The poor
Girl's underworld, a weedy thing. The night,
With its kingdom of lanterns and awful blue lark.
How we waited, how we hid
Like wolves, in the revolving question of a field.

In The Kingdom II

Toby

Spent boyhood in a ten-by-ten cabin.
Cornellian box with wings, flapping.
Bird blood, splattering. Inside,
Terror, a fire
Igniting and never not lit.
He got the gun cocked.
He got his hand on my pretty humming box.
A live machine, set forth for purring.

Nepenthe

In mother's sable, I've been
Waiting in your old room, in that
Collapse, the mishap that was
Your boyhood with its lit-globes.

Handsome in your blonde suit,
Leaning against a wall of silk
Ribbons. A blur, your pale face, a saint's
Turning away from the light.

And the hush of dusk as it slips into the hills
Like the drug of sleep. How you consumed it:
Piloting against the fenced-in night of it.
Then let it bleed—milk from the stalk.

Little Fox in Ghost-Weed

Little Fox was mine, a dappled gray pony I raced
One morning among the sweep of steeple and bindweed,

Then crashed. Fox's mouth split, and
Hoof crushed against stone.

Rocking in the ghost-weed so as not to start
The weeping.

Texarkana

Then the gun men come and then
The one in blonde fox

Clutching the Book of Ruin
In his clean, white hands.

From the barn I could see the star
Of his horse as it galloped toward us.

In the end, there was nothing
We could do.

Just watch as an ocean of bloodhounds
Flood down the side of the mountain.

Traveling Gospel

His hands were moving like twin engines
But his lips unzipped my pants.
He told me, in a voice of cold pennies,
You're the prettiest boy I have ever seen.
In a wasted field of spirit-weed, a few miles
Off the interstate, a lost trucker gentled me
With his slow song of longing. And a beautiful
Orchestra took over the milk
In my veins. A wild sky of semis
Like silver jets taking off—

Self-Portrait in Froehlichia

I was out with lanterns
When you arrived with a torch in the night.

In evening weather, I resisted.

In the evening water, I rested
A diadem of cotton
Upon the wet crown of your head.

A locket of Oklahoma summer and the blonde
Leather back seat of a stolen '68
Studebaker.

Outside the broken window,
A nodding field of rocket and a shot-
Gun of starlings, scattering.

After you vanished,
I waited for the heat to prevail.
Then I prayed.

I wish to be unhinged of all systems.
I want flocks of low-flying swan, brutal windstorm, feathered
Lamps by the thousand, dirt
In the hand. And you,

My winter, I do not believe
I imagined you might leave.
And I hope I do not
See another springtime, ever.

Microscopic Winter

We were of the West
African trees and grasses: the orchid, the flame, the quiver.

In the Nocturama of
Wild javelina, cheetah, and gazelle, we stopped
The clock for dusk. Freezing

Little Tundra, Tiny
Ice Age. Gray-crowned
Crane, with wings extended: the wool
Of your boyhood cast about your bare shoulders.

Beneath the canopy of egrets,
You slept,

Dreaming of the sea: a great ocean-
Liner, and the ripping of wind
Against the latched wing of the ship's portal.

Microscopic Winter II

You say there are no words in the English language
For the dark flocking of your sadness

And spent eleven months at sea,
Recording what you were certain
Was the light at the end of the world.

After the winter of milk-baths,
Rooms of shortwave radios
And your lifelong study of the saints,

You wrote me of the accident in father's bathroom:
The perfect slant of the blade,
And how fast it all happened.

You said you could feel the opening
Of your mind like a kingdom of light,
Then a dark bead coming at you like a black sun.

The next morning
I went up to the roof, climbed in the wire
Coop, and set your boyhood falcon free.

Toby II

Spray paint, wheat paste, home-
Made skateboard. California suburbs
Are the slums of the future. What isn't
Taken by the cops is co-opted
For endless banks of black
Television sets. And the L.A.
Sun is junk-white. Vegas-hot,
It burns the cinder block
Of the strip mall parking lot.
Someone's mother's pick-up's parked
With a glue-sniffing family
Of kids inside. And everyone is dead
In my America.

Praying I

Transfixed

Sometimes a thrasher
Enters the maelstrom.

Sometimes I remember
My brother

Before the accident.
Hiding mother's bottles in the cold blue snow.

In the distance, the house is
Fracturing. In the bedroom, the walls are

Red with racing tigers and the door is
Always locked.

Inside the ice storm, my brother
Made the sky small again.

Shoot

Into the ice-ravaged ragweed and phlox
I vanished.

Goodbye to the Ever-
Blonde Empire,

Its feather gowns and endless
Blue lanterns.

When I reached the jeweled nettle,
I abandoned

What little was left and entered
The silence in the orchard.

Shoot II

I was kneeling in the willow
When the sun fell back into its crib of poison.
The splinter floated before my eyes again.

I washed my silver handgun as I set
The last dangerous dream afloat.

The ripped yellow curtains were humming along the sill
As I entered the terrible flowering.

There isn't anything you or anyone can say.
I am my father's lost son.

You Will Be Like Your Dreams Tonight

Locked in a coop with the animals.

I went feral.
I went starboard.

I willed my mind
Into the white

Body of my brother's.
Crippled and Christ-like.

This is what it looks like to be stripped.
This is what it sounds like.

Door to Heaven

The night you left the world,
I went back to the house, that church
With the god taken out—

In father's blue plaid coat, and jet-black
Hair slicked back

Like a brother, or a summer
In the junk clinic. Back

Before you built the boat.
Before the fawn

With its star
On the forehead.

How the light collects about its temples.

And why not
Let it love me.

I spent a lifetime inside the destruction.
And like anyone, I made a world someplace else.

Secondhand Gun

There's a gunboat cutting through the distance,
Its hull ablaze with a honey light and black
Lanterns tattering in the breeze. Off the rafters
Hangs an old yellow dress I wore once when I was little.

There's a sick Shelty staring from the landing
And a pile of cages rusting in the weather.

A ghost, I enter the boat.

When it pulls up, I'll be a girl again.

Joe the Lion

Ruined at the Greyhound,
Mania, God's sweet basement
Meth, flooding every cell in your brain.
Your ticket to Cleveland
Soft with sweat and crumpled
In your small-girl hands.
Thin, then, on a music
So terrible. And black,
Your hair cut short to soft mohawk.

You knew I sold
My blood for money. And for love,
I've done things I'd rather not say.
I'd do anything not to be human,
If this is what it is.

Through the Night, Softly

Woke on the highway,
Thin in my dead brother's clothes.
I was gone but still dreaming.

A desert city strobing in the distance like sex.

In Sparks, I traded in
What little I owned
For a .22 caliber handgun.

Drunk on Seconal in the sun,
I let the poisonous helmet
Christian me.

Contrary to rumor and hearsay,
I am not dead yet.

What I recall most of that overdose
Is the gorgeous white underworld
Galloping into me.

Door to Heaven II

Already, the dream tigers have arrived.
Striped and enormous, as always.

When you vanish into the maze of silver cypress,
Let the mallow-white

Ink take the quiet
Of your mind.

Let the river
Kill the blossom.

He who hurt you once,
Shall now be put to rest.

I will find him, I will
Waste him in my own sweet way.

If I can, I will
Become you.

Praying II

January 5, 1973

Brother is harvesting my dreams again.
His skinny trailer park body
Delicate and terrible as a girl's.
Murderous, bloody-nosed brother, it was you
Who made me. I don't blame you.
You took what was given and did
What any brother would. Hollywood
Boulevard, sniffing paint from a plastic bag,
I wake dreaming on my knees again.

Sparks, Nevada

In the middle of the night, father
Brought me a falcon.

By morning, it ripped the wire and flew the hill
Into the highway.

When they found me in that car
My sleeve stemmed in blood,

I didn't know what it was
I was trying to kill.

I saw a craft of orphans streaming down the river.
They were dressed in white and silent as a séance.

It was then I spoke to the bird.

Already God is shaking his black seed
Back into me.

Prelude to 220, or 110

As a girl, I was razored
Into the world. I was never close to anyone.

World of wingless, world of hands,
I killed off everything I loved.

Do not talk to me about the stars.

I'm listening hard for the clicking
Of a river boat, cutting through

The distance, or the music of my brother
Coming back into the world, or

The sound of the night when he set
The rope in my hands, when he left

The terrible animal to me.

Through the Night, Softly II

Silver steamboat, brother.
Broken trailer wasting on the blossoming dogwood.
Towhee in the burning cotton.

What the men done
Is the cavalry come. Is the murderous
Gallop of horses.

Under the trestle
I watch the thorn bleed.
Then he dumbs me down.

Let the good
Lord drag us back to the gutter
Of his guncotton night.

You Will Be Like Your Dreams Tonight II

I discovered father's shotgun.
Dug it out from the earth like a tooth.
There was one worm in particular.
Moving, the raw pink of it
Looked like the skin of my own mouth.
I killed it with the stud of my bracelet.
Then entered the hall of the house like a son.

Joe the Lion II

Then, the great machinery begins.
The last time anybody saw you, the fawn
Walked into the field,
Night coming on like so many black wings.

Saint Francis, when he broke the wolf,
Leaned into the stinking sea of wine and blood that was
That animal's body. I am
The wolf. God is the night

I must not creep into.

Is this, then, the world:

I ask for a ship
And no ship comes.

Five-Day Locker

Past the ruin of stables and rusted cages
In Daddy's seersucker and black
Leather, I wade into the blue swamp in the river
Where all things weak break free—

Jeweled pelt of girlhood, warm
Hominy and sweet-milk, the mallow-
White billy goat
Tied by wire to the staff.

Then the Grand Duke
In Daddy's silver Mack truck
And the blonde
Crawling the endless linoleum.

What did they do to my brother
While I was under the god of their gun.

I laced my youth in medicine:
Glue and crystal
Methamphetamine. I would

Do anything
To have died, then,

With my brother
In my arms.

Transfixed II

In the legend, a gun-
Boat arrives in the night
And a boy

Leads me to a room
Where my brother is
Still breathing.

Soon,
I am riding over a blackened field of sumac
On the back of my dead pony.

Let everything weak
Die in its cage. Let God's love
Ruin me.

Capitola

I set my brother's revolver
On the earth below the willow.
I talked to the stars.

The night before
He died
I spoke with him

Of the sweet devastation
Slipping in.
I let go the bird.

I will tie my brother's goat to the staff
And drop back into the kingdom,
Calling out to everything beating.

F-Space

I buried everything you gave me
In the orchard.

Then I let the silence
Come on like a good drug.

Already, the gunboats loom.
Now the swallows

Come to me in sleep. And a boy
Whispers of Saint Francis and the wolf

He broke. In the sanitarium, some Christian brothers
Come offering solace.

But my heart is the smallest
Catafalque. Always

I was a strange sort of
Princess. Hiding in the horse-weed with my crosses.

Yellow-haired and feral in the woods.
Now, neither birds nor the sea can save me.

Set me in the field and let the stars
Have their way.

Recent Titles from Alice James Books

Alice James Books has been publishing exclusively poetry since 1973. One of the few presses in the country that is run collectively, the cooperative selects manuscripts for publication through both regional and national annual competitions. New regional authors become active members of the cooperative, participating in the editorial decisions of the press. The press, which historically has placed an emphasis on publishing women poets, was named for Alice James, sister of William and Henry, whose fine journal and gift for writing went unrecognized within her lifetime.

Typeset and Designed by Mike Burton

Printed by Thomson-Shore on 50% postconsumer recycled paper,

processed chlorine-free

৵